BRIGHTER DAYS
MUSIC AS HUMAN EXPRESSION

BY

BARBRA AKOMBO

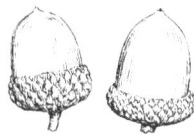

HOG PRESS

Published by
Hog Press
922 5th St.
Ames, IA 50010
USA
www.hogpress.com
editor@hogpress.com

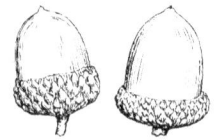

HOG PRESS

BRIGHTER DAYS: MUSIC AS HUMAN EXPRESSION
Copyright © 2016 by Barbra Achando Akombo. All rights reserved.

ISBN-13:   978-1-941892-29-9

ISBN-10:   1-941892-29-9

Table of Contents

Preface

It gives me pleasure to share with all music enthusiasts my artistic creations of these works. Music is indeed a tool for human expression. Not only does it bring joy but invigorates the soul. These four pieces *Brighter Days, The Call, Help*, and *Light* are designed to accomplish just that.

I give many thanks to my family; my mother, Sarah Ambiyo for teaching me the values of confidence, love and commitment in everything I do; my father, Prof. David. O. Akombo for inspiring me and believing in me and supporting me through my musical journey; my sister, Andrea Alali, for making me always want to be a good role models and friend; all my lecturers at Kenyatta University, especially Dr. Timothy Njoora and Mr. George Mwiruki for piano and composition lectures; my music director and friends for their inspiration. I would like to especially thank Prof. David. O. Akombo for all the mentorship he gave me in my career. An enormous debt of gratitude can hardly be repaid to my good friends, George Oduor and Joan Karanja who not only proofread multiple versions of the pieces in this book, but also provided many suggestions and substantive challenges to help me improve my music. Above all, I thank the Lord Almighty for the gift of music and the talent that sprouts within me. Yet despite all the assistance provided to me, I alone remain responsible for the content of this book, including any errors or omissions which may unwittingly remain in spite of it being a work of artistic expression. Enjoy and remember there are many more from whence these came.

Musically yours,

Barbra Akombo
Kenyatta University
Department of Music
Kenya

Brighter Days

All things come from the Lord, he is the one and on-ly God,

All things comefromtheLord, He is the one and on-ly God,

beam of the sun, dont let us burn, in - stead the yell - ow

rays, bring bright-er days. How do we tell the time is

near the wea - ther blo - ming so far from near us

these times are hard we need him here to pro - tect

thee - our spi - rit free oh - All things

come from the Lord, He is the one and on-ly God, beam of the sun, dont let us burn in-stead the yell-ow rays, bring bright-er days.

We strive so hard to do our best to make it

throu - ugh this bleak life we lead then have no

fear, the Lord is here and all things co - me from Him so

sing   All   things

come from the Lord,   He is the one and on-ly God,   beam of the sun, dont let us burn in - stead the yell-ow rays, bring bright-er days.

The Call

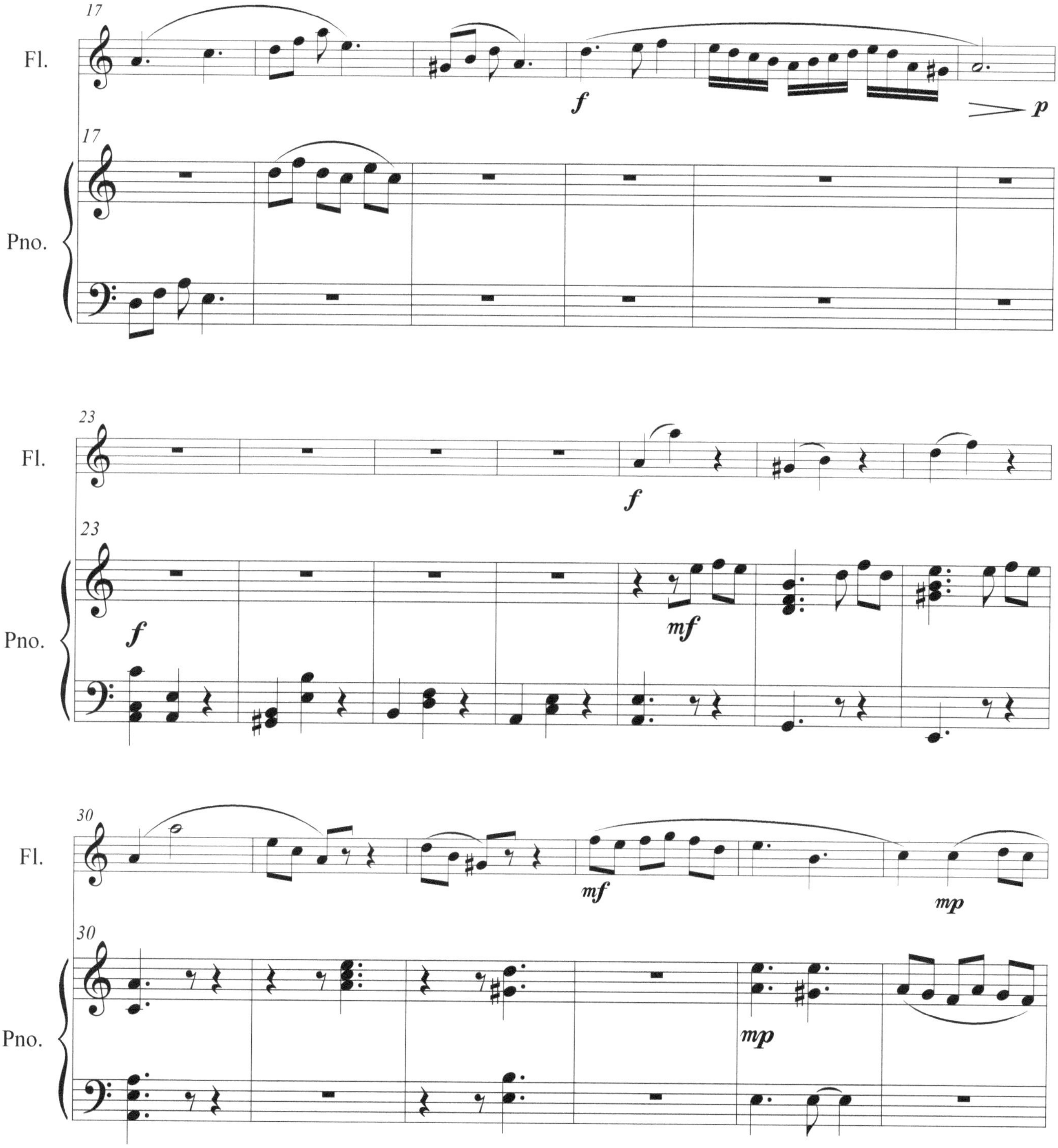
17
Fl.
f
p
Pno.
23
f
mf
30
mf
mp

© Barbra Akombo

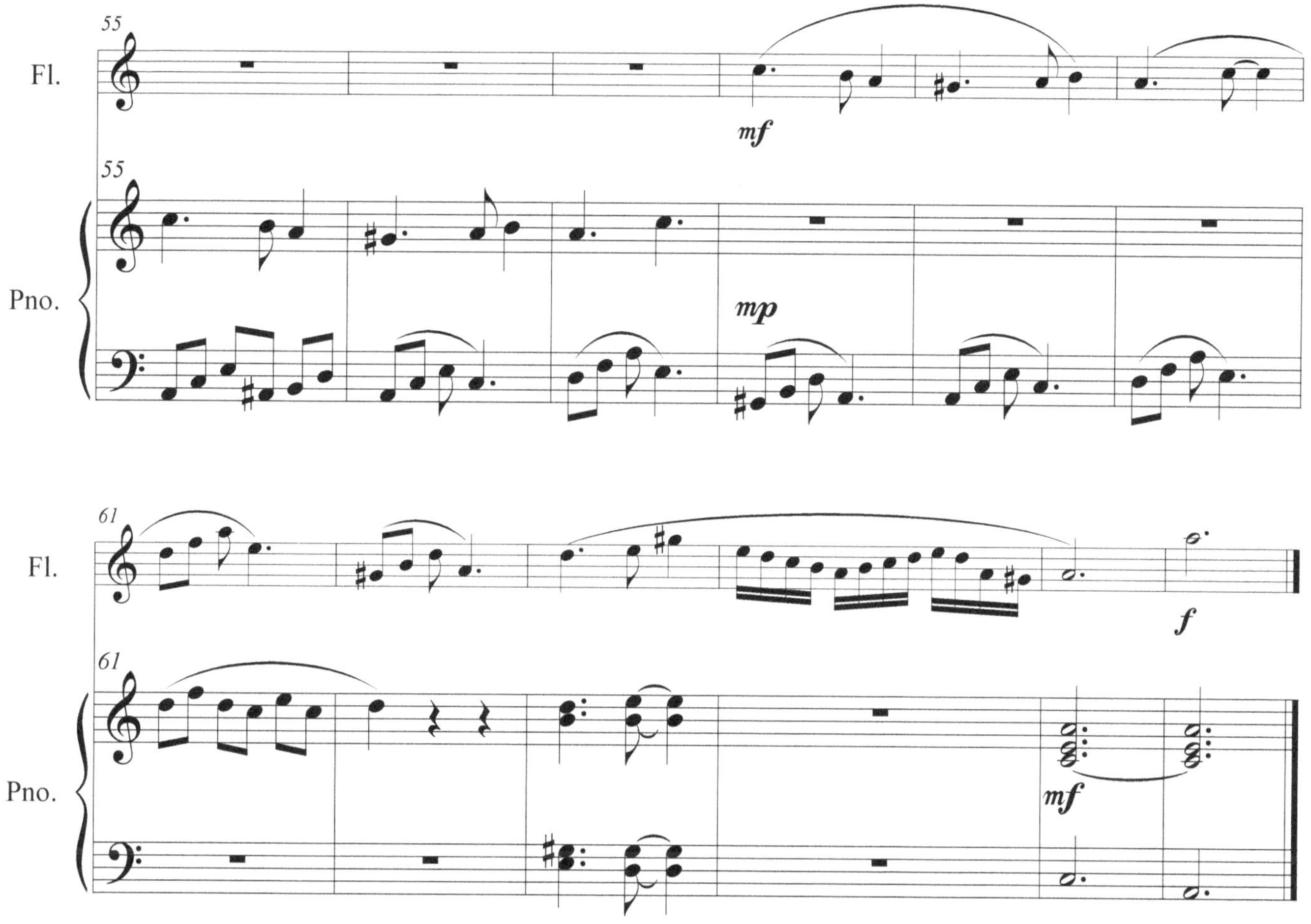
55
Fl.
mf
55
Pno.
mp
61
Fl.
f
61
Pno.
mf

Help

Moderato

Soprano: Help!___ Lord help us now ... Oh Lord!

Soprano: Help! Lord help us now___ Oh Lord!

Alto: Help! Lord he - elp help us now___ for-sake us not

S: Oh Lord we ask for your mer - cies protect those in need

S: Oh Lord we ask for your mer - cies pro - tect

A: pro - tect___ those in pro - tect

S: (Unis.) pro - tect___ those who are___ in the need___ of you - and light on their ways ev -

S: (Unis.) pro - tect___ those who are___ in the need___ of you - and light on their ways ev -

A: (Unis.) pro - tect___ those who are___ in the need___ of you - and light on their ways ev -

© Barbra Akombo

© Barbra Akombo

Measure 24 (S): Help lord! Help Lord God
Measure 24 (S): Help Lord! Help Lord
Measure 24 (A): Help Lord! Help Lord Help Lord

Measure 29 — *agitato* ... *a tempo*
(S): Help Lord! Help Lord!
(S): Help Lord! Help Lord!
(A): Help us be the ve-ry ve-ry best that we can be Help Lord!

Measure 33 — **Largo** *p*
(S): help us be the best Help Lord God! Help us be the
(S): help us be the best Help Lord! Help us be the
(A): Help Lord Help Lord!

© Barbra Akombo

S: Help us in the times when we can't un-der-stand Help Us Lord God

S: Help us in the times when we can't un-der-stand Help us Lord

A: Help us in the times when we can't un-der-stand Help us Lord

Light

Barbra Akombo

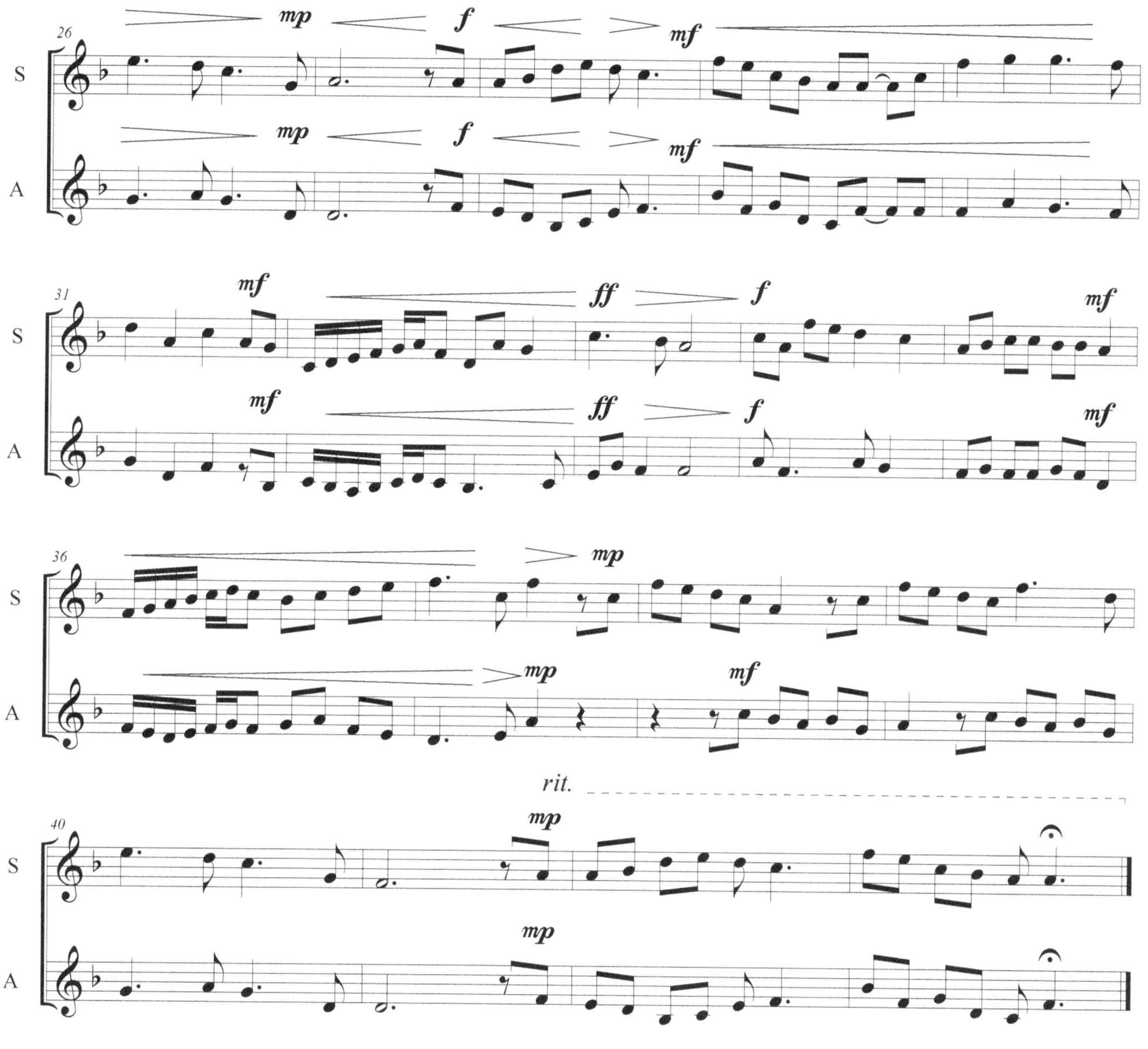
26
S
A
mp
f
mf
31
ff
36
40
rit.

Composer Biography

Barbra Akombo is a music student at Kenyatta University in Nairobi, Kenya where she is pursuing a Bachelor of Music degree. Barbra is an active member and singer with the Nairobi Music Society where she has successfully performed to an international audience such works as the *Elijah* Oratorio by Felix Mendelssohn and the Handel's *Messiah* among others. Barbara also pursues music studies with the Associated Board of the Royal Schools of Music, London, and the Kenya Music Conservatoire in Nairobi. Barbara has traveled widely, including Florence, Italy and Vienna, Austria where she has performed with the *Classical Music Festival* at The Haydnsaal Esterházy Palace in Eisenstadt, Austria.

www.ingramcontent.com/pod-product-compliance
Lightning Source LLC
Chambersburg PA
CBHW081553040426
42448CB00016B/3314